wise women wise words

Empowering
Words
of Wisdom
by Women

sonia michelson

Wise Women: Wise Words
ISBN: 978-965-7344-82-8
Copyright © 2016 Sonia Michelson

Published by

Mazo Publishers
P.O. Box 36084
Jerusalem 91360 Israel

www.mazopublishers.com
mazopublishers@gmail.com

To all my wonderful children,
grandchildren,
great grandchildren,
and students
who have also been my teachers.

Table of Contents

Introduction

Life has many ups and downs and curves. This is true for all of us. And certainly this has been true in my own life. There were many crises to live through in raising a family of seven children. And of course there were uncertainties in creating a new profession and my own teaching studio.

On the other side of the coin there have been many unexpected joys over the years from my children, students and colleagues.

Along the way, with all the ups and downs, I have been guided by wise "friends of the soul". These writings of many wise women have sustained me in both happy and sad times. Their strong voices lifted my spirits, gave me courage to keep going and to believe in my dreams.

As Eleanor Roosevelt said at age fifty-seven

"Somewhere along the line of development we discover who we really are and then we make our real decisions for which we are responsible. Make the decisions primarily for yourself because you can never really live anyone else's life, not even your own child's.

The influence you exert is through your own life, what you become by your-self. One's philosophy is not best expressed in words. It is expressed in the choices we make. In the long run, we shape our lives and we shape ourselves.

The process never ends. And the choices we make are ultimately our own responsibility."

How true these words of Eleanor Roosevelt seem to me. The key thought to remember is the power you have in making **choices**. For it is the choices you make, the thoughts you think and the words you speak that lead to and create your future. To your own individual destiny. Only you can make these choices, these decisions.

My greatest wish is for you to be inspired by these thoughts and ideas in the writings of these **Wise Women**. For your life will be richer if you take some of these thoughts to heart and make them your own. To be sure, it takes courage and determination to put thoughts into action, into deeds. But this is how you can make your dreams come true. I know this is so. For these ideas have helped me in my own life, in my own journey.

I am very grateful to my daughter Zahava Waldman for her encouragement. And especially grateful for all the time she has spent with her wonderful graphic skills in designing this book and in putting everything together in such a professional and artistic way.

In addition I appreciate the support and time spent by my sons Louis Michelson and Eliyahu Michaeli in transferring this book from the floppy disks of long ago to he present day digital format.

My love and appreciation to all three of you.

So now I want to share with you, my dear reader, some of the wisdom, knowledge and understanding that I have received during my life from these wonderful and inspiring **Wise Women** in their own words.

Sonia Michelson

Ofra, Israel
2013

Part I
The Power Of Hope

The Understanding Heart

The Essential Is Invisible

The best and most beautiful things in the world
cannot be seen or even touched.
They must be felt with the heart.
What is essential is invisible to the eye.

Helen Keller

The Good At Heart

I still believe that people
are really good at heart.

Anne Frank

A Bough In My Heart

If I keep a green bough in my heart,
the singing bird will come.

Chinese Proverb

Giving From the Heart

A well-timed home-baked chocolate cake,
a pot of chicken soup
can often soothe
many an aching heart.

Mary Pipher

The Understanding Heart

We must go to others prepared to appreciate their achievements, what they have contributed and what they still can contribute.

A warm desire to give and take, not only knowledge but sympathy and understanding - this insures that we both learn and teach "gladly".

We must learn, wherever we go before we teach. We should learn the history, ideals, ideas and attitudes or feelings of the people with whom we are working.

We must learn their language. If not the spoken language, then at least the language of the understanding heart.

Dr.Lillian Gilbreth

Hope and Happiness

Risk and Joy

Life without risk is missing
the ingredient: Joy.
If we never risk being afraid,
failing, being lonely,
we will never experience that
joy that comes from learning that
we can change ourselves.

Frances Moore Lappe

Hope

Hope
perches in the soul,
and sings,
and never stops at all.

Emily Dickinson

Dreams and the Future

The future belongs to those
who believe in the
beauty of their dreams.

Eleanor Roosevelt

Door of Happiness

When one door of happiness closes, another opens;
but often we look so long at the closed door
that we do not see the one which has been opened for us.
We could never learn to be brave and patient,
if there were only joy in the world.

Helen Keller

Hope Is the Thing With Feathers

Hope is the thing with feathers
that perches in the soul,
and sings the tune without the words,
and never stops at all.

Emily Dickinson

Happiness is Not a Vague Dream

One is happy as a result of one's own efforts.
Once one knows the necessary ingredients of
happiness -
simple tastes,
a certain degree of courage,
self-denial to a point,
love of work and
above all, a clear conscience.
Happiness is no vague dream, of that I now feel certain.

George Sand

Time and Music

The river of time
that is music,
flows through our souls
and connects us all
to one another.

Mary Pipher

Being and Becoming

Into living and learning alike, we should bring joy.
We know that we must engage again in the human dialogue.
And we should be willing, like Thoreau,
to save at the low levels and live at the high;
to pay minimum of attention to getting and spending,
and a maximum to being and becoming.

Elizabeth Monroe

To Weep and To Laugh

Those who do not know
how to weep with their
whole heart,
don't know how to laugh either.

Golda Meir

A Writer's Soul

As I reflect upon the most inspiring, helpful and exciting qualities
that books give, I think what I value most in any good book is the
opportunity to know a fine mind at work.

For writers put their best selves into their books.
Their most true selves.

In their books one becomes acquainted with their very souls, their
dreams, their experiences. What a privilege to know the minds, the
personalities, of those long dead, whom otherwise we could never
know!

Pearl S. Buck

Kindness

*One of the hardest things
to give away is
kindness.
It keeps coming back.*

Anonymous

Dreams

Dreams Within Us

Just as each cell contains
our whole being,
so each thought and dream
contains our whole self, too.
If our dreams weren't already
within us,
we could not even
dream them.

Gloria Steinem

The Human Spirit

No pessimist ever discovered the secret of the stars,
or sailed to an uncharted land,
or opened a new heaven to the human spirit.

Helen Keller

Inspiration

Inspiration comes while you are working.
Writing is a process not of **recording** *what you want to say*
but of **discovering** *what you want to say.*

View everything you do as an experiment.
The purpose of an experiment is to gather data,
to learn something you did not know before.
The beauty of viewing everything you do as an experiment is that
you can never fail.
No matter what the outcome, you will have learned either what
works or what doesn't work.
Both are extremely valuable types of information.

There is no such thing as failure,
only opportunity to learn,
grow, and renew your determination.
As the nineteenth-century theologian Soren Kierkegaard put it,
"To dare is to lose one's footing temporarily, to not dare is to lose
one's life."

Susan Page

My Highest Aspirations

Far away there in the sunshine
are my highest aspirations.
I may not reach them,
but I can look up and see their beauty,
believe in them,
and try to follow where they lead.

Louisa May Alcott

The Blue of Heaven

The blue of heaven
is larger than the clouds.

Elizabeth Barrett Browning

Young Dreams

Me
Willing to try things
Always wanting excitement
Happily content.
People
Poor, rich, old and young
Having much pride and feelings
And none are perfect.

Elise Michelson Levin (10 years old)

Love

Will To Love

To love is what gives life meaning.
The effort to understand others is the greatest manifestation of the
"will to love."
To do so, we must know what motivates people. What interests them.
What hurts them and what brings them joy.
The more aware we are, the greater our ability to make healthy
choices.

Miriam Adahan

God's Voice

Love is the
voice of God.

Grace Aquilar

Love Is Like a River

When love is strong and runs deep, it pulsates with an energy that
cannot be stopped.
When souls are connected, the relationship transcends time.
Love, like a river
flows eternal and it
embraces all those who swim in its stream.

Yitta Halberstam and Judith Leventhal

Unconditional Love

The ultimate lesson we all have to learn
is Unconditional Love,
not only others,
but ourselves as well.

Elisabeth Kubler-Ross, M.D.

Here And Now

The Here, and the Now,
and the individual have always been the special concern
of the saint, the artist, the poet and
from time immemorial - the woman.
When we start at the center of ourselves,
we discover something worthwhile
extending toward the periphery of the circle.
We find again some of the Joy in the Now
some of the peace in the Here
some of the Love in me
and that go to make up the kingdom of heaven on earth.

Anne Morrow Lindbergh

Love Is A Fruit

Love is a fruit
in season at all times,
within reach
of every hand.

Mother Teresa

Love And Compassion

The social community,
whether it be family, race
or nation is an essential of human life,
helping each individual gain security.

That person who most completely
and effectively utilizes the bonds
which link him to his fellow,
the bonds of Love and
compassion is most secure in his humanity.

Sonya Richmond

Great Love

Where there is
great love,
there are
always miracles.

Willa Cather

Forgiveness

Forgiveness Frees Us

Forgiveness frees us.
It heals our bodies and our lives.
It takes a great deal of energy
to keep someone out of our hearts.

Forgiveness moves our energy to the heart area.
Forgiveness is the initiation of the heart.
True forgiveness changes us at a core level.
It changes our bodies.
It is an experience of grace.

Christiane Northrup, M.D.

True Forgiveness

Forgiveness is an essential part of creating health.
That's because, when you don't forgive,
you have the unfinished business of your past
hanging around in your mind, body, and energy field.
And this negative energy attracts
similar hurtful situations
until you muster the courage to forgive
and change your life.

Forgiveness is a process, not an event.
Forgiveness frees you and your energy and rejuvenates your cells.
The process of true forgiveness is not simple,
but the effect of true forgiveness is essential.

So please give yourself the gift of forgiveness
for the sake of your health and your sense of peace.
And remember, sometimes the person you need to forgive
is yourself.
Don't forget to allow your heart to include you, too.

Christiane Northrup, M.D.

Forgiveness and Change

We need to forgive.
Our lives will change as a result.
Staying angry only slows down the rate of change.

Carolyn Myss, Ph.D.

Pathway to Love

Forgiveness of ourselves and of others
releases us from the past.
Forgiveness is the answer to almost everything.
I know that when we are stuck,
it usually means there is some more forgiving to be done.

When we do not flow freely with life in the present moment,
it usually means we are holding on to a past moment.
Forgiveness dissolves resentment.
Love is always the answer to healing of any sort.
And the pathway to love is forgiveness.

Louise L. Hay

Family Ties

Letting Go

Growing up under our roof,
our children (directly and obliquely) will be exposed
to our values, our styles, our views.

But letting them go eventually means
respecting their right to choose the shape of their lives.

Letting our children go,
and letting our dreams for our children go,
must be counted among our necessary losses.

And these losses are necessary
because we grow by losing and leaving and letting go.
There is a vital bond between our losses and gains.
We need to give up in order to grow.

Judith Viorst

Author's Comment

Learning how to mother myself,
while being at the same time mother to my children,
took a bit of doing.

In raising my large family of seven children
(especially when they were very little)
I found it vitally important to find some time and space
in the middle of the day to be alone.

I called this my "Hour Alone" or "My Quiet Time."

My children were wonderful.
They sensed how much this meant to me.
They intuitively understood that I had a real need for peace,
some privacy and quiet.
I read, or practiced with my guitar,
meditated or wrote in my journal.
Or just took a nap.
Unless it was a dire emergency,
no one knocked on my door or interrupted my "Hour of Quiet."
It was truly refreshing to my spirit (and my nerves)
and I returned to the fray full of energy and vitality.

I discovered early on in child raising
that if I was firm,
loving
and consistent
in my directives,
my children would (usually) come along
with the expected and hoped for behavior.

These were the key words and thoughts that kept me going:
Know my own mind,
Be firm,
Be loving and above all,
Be consistent.

Sonia Michelson

Children and Example

Bear in mind that children everywhere
have one thing in common,
they close their ears on advice
and open their eyes to example.

Anonymous

Grown Children

It is usually a surprise to find that
grown children can be delightful companions.
That doesn't mean we lose interest in others.

As writer Florida Scott Maxwell attests
from the vantage point of being 82:

"...no matter how old a mother is she watches her
middle-age children for signs of improvement..."

Gail Sheehy

Mothering Ourselves

Our culture expects mothers alone
to meet all their children's needs.

Mothering ourselves is important as mothers.
Self-sacrifice is not a healthy plan to motherhood.
Mothering ourselves takes courage!
Try it for your health's sake.

Christiane Northrup, M.D

Rainbow Mothers

There are two kinds of Mothers.
Earth Mothers nurture their children
and feed them and they thrive on this.
Society says these are "Good Mothers."

There are also creative Rainbow Mothers
who inspire their children
without necessarily having meals on the table on time.
These Mothers create that ever important nurturing home space.

Christiane Northrup, M.D.

Leaning

A Mother is not a person to lean on,
but a person to make leaning unnecessary.

Dorothy Canfield

Choosing Your Own Path

That I be not a restless ghost
who haunts your footsteps as they pass.
Beyond the point where you have left me
standing in the new spring grass.

You must be free to take a path
whose end I feel no need to know.
No irking fever to be sure
you went where I would have you go.

Those who would fence the future in
between two walls of well-laid stones
but lay a ghost walk for themselves,
a dreary walk for dusty bones.

So you can go without regret
away from this familiar land,
leaving your kiss upon my hair
and all the future in your hands.

> Margaret Mead wrote, in Blackberry Winter, that from her daughter Cathy's birth (Mary Catherine Bateson) she had tried to let her be free to choose her own path. The above poem was written to honor her daughter's 8th birthday.

The Mother Daughter Dance

A differentiated relationship between
mothers and daughters requires being who we are;

As an adult daughter,
rather than pretend,
we can show our competence
and our difficulties
and our vulnerabilities.

We, as adult daughters
can be who we are
and let Mother be who she is,

In spite of our differences,
not trying to "fix Mother up"
or change her.
Respect her for who she is
and know , as her daughter
who we are.
We are two different people.

Harriet Lerner, Ph.D

Grandparenthood

Grandparenthood can surely be a kind of
"Renaissance" experience in middle age,
with a sense of renewal,
of life beginning again.

Grandparents are usually the only people
a child will ever know in his whole life
who can give him unconditional love.
They no longer have to be disciplinarians,
that's up to the parents now.

Eda LeShan

Learning

Don't teach children.
Let them learn.

Angela Diller

Grandparent Love

Freud taught our generation of boomers
the importance of
parental love.
We know that parental love is formative,
but no one taught us about the importance of
Grandparental love.
Especially as we get older,
the bonding and nurturing go both ways.

Often grandparents can be
much more expressive with
their grandchildren
than they were with their
own children.

Connection helps our children,
our parents and us,
now and in the future.
Only by caring for our older parents
will we be able to ask our children
for help later.
And only because our children's
love of the old
will they be able to say yes to us.

Mary Pipher

On A Mother's Needs

Last year my children (ages 10 and 12) perceived
that in my relationship with colleagues and friends
I was not available to them as they would like me to be.
On an unconscious level they didn't expect me to have any needs for
friendship separate from them.

I let them know clearly that I also had needs.

Individual needs that were as important as theirs.
I came to see that I had to take a stand for my own needs
as well as the needs of my children.

Together we began working on becoming conscious
of the ways in which they didn't expect me
to have a life separate from them.
The ways we all have been socialized
to sacrifice my life for their needs.

Christiane Northrup, M.D.

Author's Comment

This quotation had special meaning for me.
It sparked a memory going back thirty years to the 1960s.

This was the time I was raising my young children.
At the same time I was trying to create a career as a music
professional. Northrup's words seemed a real validation
of what was taking place then in my own life.

When I first opened my Michelson Classical Guitar Studio at home ,
I sometimes got negative feedback from one or two of my children:
"Mommy, you like your students more than you do us!"

Of course this was not true.

This was a perception from my children's point of view.
Nevertheless, it bothered me to get this reaction.
Here's what I did.

At 10 p.m., after the last student had left my studio,
all my children came out from their rooms
where they had been studying
and we gathered around the kitchen table.
Out came the ice cream and coffee cake.

It was lots of fun as we talked, ate and had a good time together.
We were a family again with Mom at the center of things.

Sonia Michelson

Children Our Future

The solution to adult problems tomorrow
depends in large measure upon how
our children grow up today.

There is no greater insight into the future
than recognizing that when we save our children,
we save ourselves.

Margaret Mead

Family in China

The family system held us together in China.
American society does not respect the family to the same degree.
Many parents don't take the trouble
to provide discipline and guidance for their children.

Grace Zia Chu

Adolescence

Adolescence
is when children
start trying to
bring up their parents.

Anonymous

Natural Development

Flowers,
Children,
And love,
grow best
with tender care that promotes
but does not interfere with their
natural development.

Gina Allen

Part II
Living in Balance

Meditation

The Light of Insight

We meditate to discover our own identity,
our right place in the scheme of the universe.
Through meditation, we acquire and eventually acknowledge
our connection to an inner power source
that has the ability to transform our outer world.

In other words,
meditation gives us not only the light of insight
but also the power for expansive change.

Julia Cameron

Life of the Spirit

We think too much about being busy
and too little about the life of the spirit.

There is great interest in meditation now
for we are beginning to understand
that one of the severe problems in modern life
is the degree to which each of us has become
dis-connected from ourselves.

From our childhood we have been taught
to forget about our bodies and feelings and just to think.
We are heads, dis-connected from our bodies.

The new interest in meditation and sensory awareness
are attempts to reconnect the head bone to the rest of the body,
so that there can be the natural , instinctive flow
with which we were born but were soon trained to give up.

Often a frenetic pace of running
and doing becomes a running away from oneself,
from an inner sense of emptiness.

At the same time that one can look forward
with pleasurable anticipation to Doing,
it is equally important to learn to Be;
and contentment in just being with oneself.

There is really only one companion
that one can count on all through one's life,
oneself.
And that needs to be a meaningful
and satisfying friendship.

Eda LeShan

I Shall Not Live In Vain

If I can stop one heart from breaking,
I shall not live in vain:
If I can ease one life the aching,
or cool one pain,
or help one fainting robin
unto his nest again,
I shall not live in vain.

Emily Dickinson

Daily Miracles

Beautiful Mountains - Haiku

Beautiful mountains
Climbing, reaching, way above
Shyly hiding tops.

Elise Michelson Levin (age 10)

Daily Differences

We must not, in trying to think about how we can make a big
difference, ignore the small daily differences we can make which,
over time, add up to the big differences that we often cannot foresee.

Marion Wright Edelman

Living Each Day to the Fullest

It is only when we truly know and understand that we have a limited time on earth, and that we have no way of knowing when our time is up, that we will begin to live each day to the fullest; as if it was the only one we had.

Elisabeth Kubler-Ross, M.D.

Improve the World

How wonderful it is that nobody need wait a single moment before starting to improve the world.

Anne Frank

The Earth

It is a wholesome and necessary thing for us
to turn again to the earth and
in the contemplation of her beauties
to know of wonder and humility.

Rachel Carson

Coincidences

Coincidences are the miracles
in which God prefers to remain anonymous.

Doris Lessing

Open Your Heart

Coincidences are everywhere and can happen at any time
when your Soul is ready they will come.
All that is required is that you open your heart.

Yitta Halberstam and Judith Leventhal

Miracles of God

The miracles of God are truly wondrous.
Our perceptions are constantly made finer,
so that our eyes can see and our ears can hear
what is there about us always.

Willa Cather

Beauty Blooms

For it is only framed in space that beauty blooms.
Only in space are events and objects and people unique and
significant, and therefore beautiful.
A tree has significance if one sees it against the empty face of the sky.
A note in music gains significance from the silences on either side.
Even small and casual things take on significance
if they are washed in space,
like a few autumn grasses in one corner
of an Oriental painting,
the rest of the page bare.

Anne Morrow Lindbergh

Friendship

Friendship and Growth

*A friend
is someone who leaves you with
all your freedom intact,
but who obliges you to be fully
what you are.*

Anonymous

Friendship With Oneself

*Friendship with oneself is
all important,
because without it
one cannot be friends
with anyone else in the world.*

Eleanor Roosevelt

Friends in Spots

*Psychoanalyst McMahon writes that "growth demands relatedness
and that intimacy produces continuing growth throughout life,
because 'being known' affirms and strengthens the self."*

He quotes philosopher Martin Buber,

> *"All real living is meeting between I and Thou,
> and that through the Thou,
> through close encounter in which we open ourselves to each
> other, a man becomes an I."*

*Close friends contribute to our personal growth. And they care.
They come when we call, they lend us a bed, a car, an ear and this
involves rights and obligations.*
*They enrich our emotional life. They shelter us from loneliness.
For although we are taught to value self-sufficiency (and there may
be an inner core that we may never reveal),*
*it matters to us enormously that we matter to others and that we
are not alone.*
For as George Santayana wrote:

> *"Friendship is almost always the union of a part of one mind
> with a part of another; people are friends in spots."*

Judith Viorst

A New World Is Born

Each friend represents a world in us,
a world possibly not born
until they arrive.
And it is only by this meeting
that a new world is born.

Anais Nin

Obligation in Friendship

In this world you will have to make your own way.
To do that you must have friends.
You can make friends by being honest
and you can keep them by being steadfast.

You must keep in mind that friends worth having
will in the long run
expect as much from you
as they give to you.

Letter to Andrew Jackson from his Mother

Worth of Friends

I learned the true worth of all my best friends
when I turned to them.
Or, to be totally accurate,
my best friends turned to me.

They turned and offered sheltering arms,
companionship, sympathetic ears,
and a love that makes no demands.

They were there in 1988.
They were there before I even knew Lee.
They are still there.
And there are new friends, too,
friends who never even met Lee.

Lois Wyse

Loving Wholeheartedly

*There is nothing I would not do for those
who are really my friends.
I have no notion of loving people by halves.*

Jane Austen

Friendship and Hope

*Sometimes it is a slender thread,
sometimes a strong, stout rope;
She clings to one end,
I the other.*

*She calls it friendship.
I call it hope.*

Lois Wyse

Friendship Takes Time

Nobody sees a flower – really,
it is so small.
It takes time.
We haven't time.
And to see,
takes time.

Like to have a friend,
takes time.

Georgia O'Keeffe

A True Friend

A friend is one
who knows you as you are,
understands where you've been,
accepts who you've become,
and still gently invites you
to grow.

Anonymous

Groups of Friends

One thing that American society lacks, from my point of view, is
that people don't have groups of friends.
You have one individual friend.
And if something happens to him or her, you have no one to talk too.
And you wind up at the psychiatrist's office.

I think you have to have people you can depend on.
I have friends who let me talk things out.
Through the talking I realize what I must do.

Grace Chu (at age 80)

Love Me Please

Love me please.
I love you.
I can bear to be your friend.

Edna St. Vincent Millay

Hug Your Friend

The only thing to do
is to hug one's friend tight
and do one's job.

Edith Wharton

Communication Between Friends

There was nothing remote or mysterious here,
only something private.

The only secret was the ancient communication
between two people.

Eudora Welty

Kindness

Guard within yourself that treasure,
kindness.
Know how to give without hesitation,
how to lose without regret,
how to acquire without meanness.

Know how to replace in your heart,
by the happiness of those you love,
the happiness that may be wanting to yourself.

George Sand

Self Esteem

Preparation and Self-Reliance

*If you prepare yourself at every point in life as well as you can,
with whatever means you may have,
you will be able to grasp opportunity for broader experience when it
appears.*

*Without preparation you cannot do it.
The lessons we learn in life should teach us adaptability and
adjustment.
And finally of self-reliance and developing into an individual as
every human being must.*

*Life was meant to be lived and curiosity must be kept alive.
One must never, for whatever reason, turn his back on life.*

> Eleanor Roosevelt

Become Someone Alone

To restore color to our faded personalities and
vitality to our languid minds,
we must learn to do things,
to think things,
to become some one alone.

Mary Ellen Chase

Unique Handwriting

Just as each violinist drawing a bow across they strings of his
instrument has his individual,
unique way of bowing,
which determines the essential quality of expression of his tone,
so each individual has his unique manner of tracing a stroke in his
handwriting.

Klara Roman

Strength

Everything nourishes
what is strong already.

Jane Austen

Fashion From The Inside-Out

Our approach to dressing, make up, hair and personal care is to
find out who you are, then do it on purpose.
If we can find out who we are on the inside,
we can express it on the outside.

I've decided that I like to wear skirts that are long and warm
and I don't care what the season's length is.
I've developed a personal style in clothing that suits me
and that is not subject to the whims of the fashion designers.

I've healed my relationship with fashion, clothing and style
by first becoming comfortable with who I am.
I call this "fashion from the inside out."

Christiane Northrup, M.D.

I See Beyond

Like Henry David Thoreau, the famed mystic of Walden Pond,
Amelia Earhart could say.

> *"I hear beyond the range of sound,*
> *I see beyond the range of sight,*
> *New earth and skies and seas around."*

Amelia Earhart

Your Consent

No one can make you
feel inferior
without your consent.

Eleanor Roosevelt

Try A Certain Job

Try a certain job, and if you find that you are the first woman
to feel an urge in that direction---what does it matter?

Feel it, and act on it just the same.
It may turn out to be fun, and to me fun is the indispensable part of
work.

Amelia Earhart

Dignity of Each Individual

Man's humanity lies in the recognition that
who one is can transcend one's gifts and achievement.

The sense that each individual represents one aspect of humanity
with a dignity all its own.

Hannah Arendt

Love and Lovable

The conviction of being loved and lovable,
valued and valuable as we are,
regardless of what we do,
is the beginning of the most
fundamental self-esteem.

Gloria Steinem

True Identity

I believe true identity is found in creative activity
springing from within.
It's found paradoxically,
when one loses ones self.

Women can best re-find herself
by losing herself
in some kind of creative activity
of her own.

Anne Morrow Lindberg

Self Evaluation

There is no pleasing everyone, as we all know.

The truth is, that when you please yourself,
you usually end up pleasing other people, too.

They will sense in you integrity and your sense of fulfillment.
And this will enhance their lives and give them stimulus to do the
same.

Other people accept the evaluation you put on yourself.

> Marie Edward and E. Hoover

Respect Yourself

In personal conduct always be polite,
but never obsequious.
No one will respect you more
than you esteem yourself.

> Letter to President Andrew Jackson
> from his Mother

Core Self-Esteem

Of course everything is a journey,
and nothing is a destination.

But it seems to be true, once we are past the
early stages of absorbing parental love,
some core of self-esteem is a vital preface
to allow ourselves to be fully loved by others.

Gloria Steinem

True Emancipation

True Emancipation begins
neither at the polls
nor in the courts.
It begins in woman's soul.

Emma Goldman

1911

Self Respect

When you have self-respect, you have enough.
And when you have enough, you have self-respect.

Fortunately, because there are always people
and events to stretch us,
none of us needs worry about falling
into self-satisfied sloughs of "absolute" maturity.

Gail Sheehy

Discipline

Life and Discipline

Without discipline,
there's no life at all.

Katherine Hepburn

Discipline of Mind and Body

Discipline of mind and body
is one of the most
difficult things one has to acquire.

But in the long run
it is a valuable ingredient of education,
and a tremendous bulwark in time of trouble.

Discipline is essential in meeting defeats
and recovering from disaster.

Eleanor Roosevelt

Consciousness

The difficulties that come to you are exactly in proportion to your strength.

*Nothing can happen which does not belong to your consciousness,
and all that belongs to your consciousness you are able to master.*

> Anonymous

Genius and Discipline

*Genius at first
is little more than
a capacity for
receiving discipline.*

> George Eliot

The Little Things

He that neglects
the little things,
shall fail little by little.

Hebrew Proverb

Hard Work and Good Fortune

If you want to be the best, it's just plain work.
My singing came first and I learned how to sacrifice.
If I hadn't stuck to the principles established by my father,
I wouldn't be singing today.

Yes, I've had some luck along the way
but hard work enabled me to take advantage of good fortune.

Marilyn Horne

Patient Practice

When an artist has been able to say,
"I came, I saw, I conquered,"
it has been at the end of patient practice.

George Eliot

Getting Down To Work

I don't wait for moods.
You accomplish nothing if you do that.
Your mind must know it has got to get down to work.

Pearl S. Buck

Perseverance

What they took for inattentiveness
was a miracle of concentration.

Toni Morrison

Using Time Wisely

Author's Comment

Using time wisely has always been a major concern of mine, and of course, of yours.
There always seems so much to do, so many demands on our time and so little time to do it all.

The first time I became aware of time and how to use it wisely was in reading a slender volume given to me by my father many years ago, "How To Live on Twenty-Four Hours A Day" by Arnold Bennett, which was first published in 1910.

On first reading this seemed like a very old fashioned book. Of course I was only 17 at the time.
What did I know? And it was so very, very British. Over the years I've returned to this book and each re-reading brings fresh insights.

He mentions the miracle of just 24 hours a day that each of us has. Do we use this miracle of time wisely or as he puts it "do we just muddle through?" And then he goes on to point out ways to use our time wisely.

He does caution that this will take effort and the "tense bracing of the will" before anything worth doing can be done. And adds with a bit of a twinkle in his eye "I rather like it myself. I feel it to be the chief thing that differentiates me from the cat by the fire."

And he does indicate that controlling one's mind is the first element of a full existence. "People say: 'One can't help one's thoughts.' But one can."

I also like what Alan Lakein has to say in his "How to Get Control of Your Time and Your Life." Mr. Lakein is a well known time management consultant and has lots of good ideas about using your time wisely in today's world. One of my favorites is the following advice:

"I remind myself: 'there is always time for the important things.' If it is important, I'll make time to do it."

Sonia Michelson

Timely Advice

1. *Achieve inner calm.*
   Maintain peace within yourself so that much can go on around you and you can stay calm inwardly and outwardly. Having the ability to attain calm regardless of outside turmoil is a kind of strength. With this strength one can work undisturbed by what goes on around one.

2. *Concentrate on the thing at hand.*
   Give your full attention. Then be able to put it aside and go on to the next thing without confusion.

3. *Organize your time.*
   Arrange a routine pattern that allots certain activities to certain hours, planning in advance for everything that must be done. At the same time try remaining flexible enough to allow for the unexpected.

4. *Use common sense in health.*
   By using your common sense you will be able to rely on your energy when most needed. Self-discipline is most important to be able to regulate life and habits in a sensible way.

   Eleanor Roosevelt

The Worth of Time

Have regular hours for work and play.
Make each day both useful and pleasant.
Prove that you understand the worth of time by employing it well.

Then youth will be delightful,
old age will bring few regrets,
and life will become a beautiful success.

Louisa May Alcott

Health and Healing

Wisdom of the Body

By wisdom of the body, I mean that we must learn to trust that the symptoms in the body are often the only way the soul can get our attention.

Covering up our symptoms with external "cures" prevents us from "healing" the parts of our lives that need attention and change.

Christiane Northrup, M.D.

Taking Care of Yourself

To take good care of yourself,
you need a daily routine that includes

> *Meditation*
> *Exercise*
> *Good food and good hygiene*
> *Right amount of rest*
> *Home*
> *Personal challenge*
> *Relaxation and pleasure*
> *Friends.*

Mix in with these a good amount of love,
and you will reap great rewards.

Barbara Ann Brennan

Inner Guidance

Only our connection with our own inner guidance and our emotions
is reliable in the end.
We each comprise a multitude of processes that have never existed
before and never will again.
Science must acknowledge truthfully how much it doesn't know and
leave room for mystery, miracles and the wisdom of nature.
Pay attention to them

Christiane Northrup, M.D.

Author's Comment

As Deepak Chopra , M.D., said in "Creating Health",
"You are what you think. For every state of consciousness, there is a
corresponding state of physiology."
It took me a long time to realize the truth of the mind/body
connection.
If my shoulder or back aches maybe I need to slow down and take a
break?
Get away from writing and my computer.
Then I may go and water my plants. Maybe I'll do a I little
gardening. Go outside and get some fresh air. It's a change of pace.

Before I realize it perhaps my shoulder or back ache goes away.

Maybe my mind is going around and around with lots of energy .
Maybe I need to take a break from writing.

OK. So it's time to get on my stationary bike and work off some
cerebral steam.

Or perhaps I need to do some deep breathing exercises ,which I
learned from reading books by Dr. Andrew Weil .

And then, if time permits, I sit and meditate for a few minutes.
Slow down, slow down, I tell myself.
So for me, the mindbody connection is really one word.
And it is very important to understand this concept.
Being grounded, having clarity of mind and purpose
are goals we all want in our busy daily lives.

Sonia Michelson

Eating Mindfully

Eat Mindfully and enjoy your food fully.

1. *Eat sitting down.*

2. *Taste the food, savor it, assimilate it. Then you won't be tempted to eat more, to fill up ... the "nourishment void."*

3. *Eat a favorite food without reading a book or watching TV.*

4. *Slow down: consider the fact that you can enjoy only the food that is in your mouth at the moment.*

5. *Be fully engaged in the process of self-nourishment and your food will be metabolized in the right way.*

6. *Pay attention to the taste of the food and the experience of eating. Be Present!*

   Christiane Northrup, M.D.

Energy Medicine

You are a latticework of energies.
The enormous implications of this single fact
are the basis of energy medicine.
Much as fluctuations in tone and tempo
form the vocabulary of music.
So the more fluent you become in sensing the
shared vocabulary of mind, body and soul
the more skillfully you can orchestrate
their lifelong symphony.

Donna Eden

Steps for Healing

1. *Get your history straight, i.e. your medical, social and family history.*

2. *Sort through your beliefs. Do you believe you can be healthy?*

3. *Respect and release your emotions.*

4. *Learn to listen to your body.*

5. *Learn to respect your body.*

6. *Acknowledge a Higher Power or Inner Wisdom.*

7. *Get help with a skilled listener.*

8. *Work with the body.*

9. *Gather information, read, read, read!*

10. *Reclaim the fullness of your mind.*

11. *Forgive.*

12. *Actively participate in your life.*

Christiane Northrup, M.D.

Inner Guidance

By wisdom of the body,
I mean that we must learn to trust
that the symptoms in the body are often
the only way the soul can get our attention.
Covering up our symptoms with external "cures"
prevents us from "healing" the parts of our lives
that need attention and change.

Only our connection with our own inner guidance
and our emotions is reliable in the end.
We each comprise a multitude of processes
that have never existed before and never will again.

Science must acknowledge truthfully
how much it doesn't know and
leave room for mystery, miracles and the wisdom of nature.
Pay attention to them.

Christiane Northrup, M.D.

Part III
Renaissance In Mid-Life

Making Choices

Making Real Decisions

Somewhere along the line of development we discover who we really are, and then we make our real decision for which we are responsible.
Make that decision primarily for yourself because you can never really live anyone else's life, not even your own child's.
The influence you exert is through your own life and what you become yourself.

Eleanor Roosevelt

Well Being

Like the dance of a brilliant reflection on a clear pond,
well being is a shimmer that accumulates from many
important life choices
made over the years by a mind that is not often muddied by
pretense or ignorance,
and a heart that is open enough
to sense people in their depths and
to intuit the meaning of most situations.

Gail Sheehy

Game of Life

One receives only that
which is given.

The game of life is a
game of boomerangs.

Our thoughts, deeds, and words,
return to us sooner or later,
with astounding accuracy.

Florence Scovel Shin

Using Change Effectively

The essence of whether one experiences " Renaissance"
or "the Dark Ages" in middle life,
seems to me to depend a great deal on the degree
to which one can use change effectively,
rather than denying its existence
and trying to get on with business as usual.

The most unhappy of the middle-aged and older
seem to be those who cannot change.

It seems to me that we have some very important choices to make.
And even 'doing nothing' is a choice.
Continued years of fulfillment
are almost entirely dependent on how well we choose.

Eda LeShan

Choices We Make

One's philosophy is not best expressed in words;
it is expressed in the choices one makes.

In the long run, we shape our lives and we shape ourselves.
The process never ends.

And the choices we make are ultimately our
own responsibility.

Eleanor Roosevelt

Myriad Moments

Every day is made from myriad moments.
In each of these moments we have choices.

Julia Cameron

New Beginnings

We often overlook many options because they seem unimportant,
but even one small, seemingly inconsequential decision
can either limit or expand the possibilities for other choices.

George Eliot, the British novelist, wrote in one of her books that
"the strongest principle of growth lies in human choice."

It is amazing how well other people can rally
when we insist on having our own lives.
To think that we are indispensable is the height of egotism.
We are indispensable to our own lives,
and we must begin to choose to live those lives
or we will despair and die.

To the degree that we make this choice,
the next twenty or thirty years can be the most fulfilling of our lives.
We need to take a chance on new beginnings.

Eda LeShan

Shedding Shells

Perhaps middle age is, or should be, a period of shedding shells;
the shell of ambition,
the shell of material accumulations and possessions,
the shell of the ego.

Perhaps one can shed at this stage in life, one's pride, one's mask.
Perhaps one can at last in middle age be completely oneself.
And what a liberation that would be!

Anne Morow Lindbergh

Important Decisions

No trumpets sound when the important decisions of our life are made.
Destiny is made known silently.

Agnes De Mille

Who We Are

Service is small and quiet
and everywhere.
Far more often we serve by
who we are
and not what we know.
And everyone serves whether
they know it or not.

Many simple, ordinary things
we do can affect those around us
in profound ways.

- *the unexpected phone call*
- *the brief touch*
- *the willingness to listen generously*
- *the warm smile*
- *the gracious welcome*
- *to really pay attention*

Rachel Naomi Remen, M.D.

Responsible For Our Choices

I believe that we are solely responsible for our choices,
and we have to accept the consequences
of every deed,
word, and
thought throughout our lifetime.

Elisabeth Kubler-Ross

Courage

Have courage.
One's life shrinks or expands
in proportion to one's courage.

Anais Nin

Brave Women

I have met brave women who are exploring the outer edge
of human possibility,
with no history to guide them, and
with courage to make themselves vulnerable
that I find moving beyond words.

Gloria Steinem

New Steps

The courage to take new steps allows us to let go of each adult stage
with its satisfactions
and to find the fresh responses that will release the richness of the
next stage.

As Dostoevsky put it, "Taking a new step, uttering a new word, is
what people fear most."

The real fear should be of the opposite course.
The power to animate all of life's stages and seasons
is a power that resides within us.

Gail Sheehy

Strong Women

I long to speak out
the intense inspiration
that comes to me
from the lives of strong women.

Ruth Benedict

Helping to Change the Current Culture

We have to face the fact that striving for a whole self means going
against - and thus helping to change - most of our current culture.
However great the struggle, the rewards are even greater.

Gloria Steinem

How High We Are

*We never know how high we are
till we are called to rise.
And then if we are true to plan
our statures touch the skies.*

Emily Dickinson

Take Courage

*Be strong,
and let your heart take courage.*

Psalms 31:25

Suffering

*Although the world is full of suffering,
it is also full of the overcoming of it.*

Helen Keller

Light

We have enough light given to us to guide our own steps.

George Eliot

Spirit of Courage

When you have no choice,
mobilize the spirit of courage.

Jewish Proverb

Difficult Duty

To every difficult duty is a charm,
known only to those who have the courage to undertake it.

Madame Swetchine

Exertion and Courage

Courage and exertion.
These seem to be the weapons
with which we must fight life's long battle.

Charlotte Bronte

Talent and Art

True strength is delicate.
Courage is the difference between
talent and art.

Louise Nevelson

Second Birth

Every artist makes himself born.
It is very much harder the other time,
and longer.

Willa Cather

To Be An Individual

It is a brave thing to have courage,
to be an individual.
It is also, perhaps, a lonely thing.
But it is better than not being an individual,
which is to be nobody at all.

Eleanor Roosevelt

Respect Yourself

It takes courage to learn to respect yourself
and your body,
regardless of how wounded you've been,
regardless of your current weight,
regardless of your personal relationships.
Commit to living your dreams!
One day at a time.
This is the process that is required
to heal our families and our planet.

Christiane Northrup, M.D.

To Be Someone Different

There are few personalities strong enough
to maintain a style of life peculiar to themselves alone.

To break away from the pattern of one's group,
to be someone different,
to follow one's own bent,
to write one's own hand-
-this calls for courage.

This calls for courage of an independent mind
and some creative potential and originality.

It is a most impressive observation
that the same personal style appears consistently
in all aspects of an individual's activity.

The manner of expression that is seen in his handwriting
is found likewise in his speech,
his gesture's and his gait,
his thoughts and his creative work.

Klara G. Roman

Believe You Can Achieve

Most people are conditioned to accept the idea of limitation.
And I am firmly convinced that the concept of limitation originates
entirely in the mind,
either your own or that of someone
who has had influence over you.
Do not accept anyone else's idea of what you can do.
Anything you believe you can achieve, you can achieve.

     Nancy Roberts

Follow Your Heart

If you follow the inner desire of your heart,
the incidentals will take care of themselves.
Women can do most of the things men can do.
In anything that requires intelligence, coordination,
spirit, coolness, and will power,
women can meet men on their own ground.

     Amelia Earhart

Courage to Face Change

Have courage to face change.
Don't be afraid to give up the old life.

With new spiritual power and understanding
profound changes will occur.
Understand and accept them.

The butterfly must leave the larva life
and venture into a form totally different
and until them, unknown to him.
It must participate in a struggle to emerge
into a beautiful, fantastically different
creature of its new life.

Jo Anne Chase

Remaining Whole Midst Distractions

The problem is not merely one of woman and career,
woman and the home, woman and independence.
It is more basically: how to remain whole
in the midst of the distractions of life.
How to remain balanced, no matter what centrifugal forces
tend to pull one off center.
How to remain strong, no matter what shocks come in at
the periphery and tend to crack the hub of the wheel.

Anne Morrow Lindbergh

Sound of Wings

Courage is the price that Life exacts for granting peace.
The soul that knows it not
knows no release from little things.
Knows not the livid loneliness of fear,
nor mountain heights where bitter joy can hear
the sound of wings.

How can life grant us boon of living,
compensate for dull gray ugliness and pregnant hate,
unless we dare the soul's dominion?
Each time we make a choice,
we pay with courage
to behold the restless day,
and count it fair.

Amelia Earhart

Creativity

To Begin Again

Creativity is the ability to put old material into new form.
And it is only when old molds, and old ways of doing things
are forcibly broken up by need or suffering,
compelling us to re-group, to re-think,
to begin again, that the creative process starts to flow.

Catherine Marshall

The Right To Be Different

I don't want to settle for being ordinary,
and in some ways, middle age seems to be the very best time of life.
I feel I have earned the right to be eccentric.
I am being facetious about eccentricity,
but it has a deeper meaning for me.

It involves really,
the right to be different,
and therefore to be creative!

I recently saw a poster on creativity:
The man who follows the crowd
will usually get no further than the crowd.
The man who walks alone is likely to find himself
in places no one has ever been before.

Creativity in living is not without its attendant difficulties,
for peculiarity breeds contempt.
And the unfortunate thing about being ahead of your time
is that when people finally realize you were right,
they'll say it was obvious all along.

You have two choices in your life.
You can dissolve into the mainstream
or you can be distinct.
To be distinct, you must be different.
To be different, you must strive to be
what no one else but you can be.

Trusting oneself is a most important key
to discover who one is and what one wants to be.
The better we know our real selves,
the more we can let life happen to us.

The more we can trust our perceptions,
our wishes, our courage to meet life
with an open heart,
without needing to have life
programmed for us,
we can then take full responsibility for our own lives.

Eda LeShan

Creative Work

We are traditionally rather proud of ourselves
for having slipped creative work in there
between the domestic chores and obligations.
I'm not sure we deserve such big A pluses for that.

Toni Morrison

Our Second Birth

Individual growth is important.
The collective and the individual are inseparable.
Society needs both.

Artistic creativity begins with what Jung called "our second birth".
That is, giving birth
to ourselves after our natural birth.

There is a "man, woman and child within ourselves," as Beaudelaire
said, and the child is usually an orphan
and requires much attention.

Anais Nin

Creative Minds

Creative minds have always been known
to survive any kind of bad training.

Anna Freud

Creativity and Spirituality

Creativity is an experience, to my eye,
a spiritual experience.
It does not matter which way you think of it:
creativity leading to spirituality
or spirituality leading to creativity.

As Carl Jung answered the question of belief late in life.
"I don't believe; I know."

Julia Cameron

Growth and Maturity

Coming of Age

A woman must come of age by herself.
She must find her true center alone.
This lesson seems to need re-learning
about every twenty years in a woman's life.

Anne Morrow Lindbergh

Growth

The truth is that,
like every other part of nature,
human beings have
an internal imperative to grow.

Gloria Steinem

On Blessing Life

Blessing life moves us closer to each other
and closer to our authentic selves.
When people are blessed they discover
that their lives matter,
that there is something in them
worthy of blessing.

And when you bless others
you discover the same thing
is true about yourself.

We do not serve the weak
or the broken.
What we serve is the wholeness
in each other
and the wholeness in life.

Unlike helping and fixing
and rescuing
service is mutual.

There are many ways to serve
and strengthen the life around us.

- *through friendship*
- *or parenthood*
- *or work*
- *by kindness*
- *by compassion*
- *by generosity*
- *or acceptance*
- *through our philanthropy*
- *our example*
- *our encouragement*
- *our beliefs*

No matter how we do this,
our service will bless us.

Rachel Naomi Remen, M.D.

Ambiguity

Maturity is the ability
to live with ambiguity.

Barbara B Seaman

Life Force

As we get older, we have to work harder and harder
at mobilizing the life-force within each of us.
And what that seems to mean
is being as clear as we can be
about who we are.

One's unique identity as a human being
is the force, the vitality
that makes life worth living.

Eda LeShan

What You Need

You always get what you need,
not what you want.
And as you grow and evolve,
you get more.

Not when you want it,
but when you are ready for it.

Elisabeth Kubler-Ross, M.D.

Change

Life is measured by
the rapidity of
change.

George Eliot

Life As A Pilgrimage

I see my life as a pilgrimage and growth process.
I don't see one achievement as greater than another.
As far as I'm concerned,
they are steps along the process of growth.

Hopefully, my life will have touched somebody else's.
The real contribution that older women can make
to younger women
is to give them a sense of continuity.

Pauli Murray

Growth in Consciousness

Perhaps the greatest progress, humanly speaking,
in these past twenty years for both women and men,
is in the growth of consciousness.:

Of the dignity and rights of an individual,
regardless of race, creed, class or sex.
The questioning of the materialistic values of the Western world.

A new consciousness of our place in the universe,
and a new awareness of the interrelatedness
of all the life on our planet.

Much of the exploration and new awareness
is uncomfortable and painful for both men and women.
Growth in awareness has always been painful,
but it does lead to greater independence,
and eventually, cooperation in action.

For the enormous problems that face the world today,
both in the private and the public sphere,
cannot be solved by women or by men alone.
They can only be surmounted by men and women side by side.

Anne Murrow Lindbergh

Say Yes To The Unknown

As for who we will be,
the answer is:
we don't know.

We are on the edge of history.
But we do know that
growth comes from saying
Yes
to the unknown.

Gloria Steinem

People Change

People change and
forget to tell each other.

Lillian Hellman

Emotionally Mature

One of the positive aspects
of my psychotherapy
was that I came
to value myself more and more.

As I was able to express myself
in more creative ways,
I became more interesting
to myself to be with!.

Further, as I became
more mature emotionally,
I could Mother myself
more effectively.

I could feel safer and more secure
in my own company.
I knew that here was someone present
who could take care of me----me.

Eda LeShan

Passages

*It would be surprising
if we didn't experience some pain
as we leave the familiarity
of one adult stage
for the uncertainty of the next.*

*But the willingness
to move through each passage
is equivalent to the
willingness to live abundantly.*

*If we don't change,
we don't grow.
If we don't grow,
we are not really living.*

Gail Sheehy

Acceptance

Just as we must learn to accept
the limitations of others,
so we must learn never
to demand of someone else
what is not freely offered to us.
It is a form of spiritual blackmail.

What is freely given in love
and affection or companionship
one should rightly rejoice in.
But what is withheld one must not demand.

So it is a major part of maturity
to accept not only your own shortcomings
but those of the people you love,
and to help them not to fail.

Eleanor Roosevelt

Flexibility of Mind

A well-adjusted person
is able to expand his way of thought
to meet reality.
We must try to cultivate
flexibility of mind.

Sonya Richmond

Change

Change is the manifestation
of our ability to grow and become.
When it occurs to those
nearest and dearest to us
it is an opportunity for celebration.

When it happens in ourselves,
it allows us to share
ourselves on a new level.

Anne W. Schaef

Success

Life As An Adventure

Life is either
a daring
adventure
or nothing.

Helen Keller

Success

Success must include two things:
The development of an individual
to her utmost potentiality,
and a contribution
of some kind to the world.

Eleanor Roosevelt

Your Self and Your Work

The one important thing
I have learned over the years
is the difference
between taking one's work seriously
and taking one's self seriously.

The first is imperative
and the second is disastrous.

Margot Fonteyn

Necessity

Ambition is not enough;
necessity is everything.

Martha Graham

Intuition

Intuition is the direct perception of truth or fact
independent of any reasoning process.
To use intuition
is simply to use more of our intelligence
than we are accustomed to using.

Our bodies are designed to function best
when we are doing work
that feels exactly right for us,
then our health is enhanced.

If we want to know God's will for us,
all we have to do
is look to our own gifts and talents.
That's where we will find it.

We get excited and are inspired automatically
by these thoughts and feelings
which in turn keep us in touch with inner knowing
and spiritual energy.
The result is enthusiasm and joy

Christiane Northrup, M.D.

Do The Best You Can Every Day

You really can change the world if you care enough.
If you don't like the way the world is,
you can change it.
You just do it one step at a time.

Service is what life is all about.
You are not obligated to win.
You are obligated to keep trying.
You do the best you can every day.

Marion Wright Edelman

Character

Character cannot be developed in ease and quiet.
Only through experience of trial and suffering
can the soul be strengthened,
ambition inspired,
and success achieved.

Helen Keller

Commencement Address

I'm a novelist.
My work is human nature.
Real life is all I know.

Don't ever confuse the two,
your life and your work.
The second is only part of the first.

You walk out of here this afternoon
with only one thing that no one else has.
You will be the only person
who has sole custody of your life.

Your particular life.
Your entire life.

Not just your life at a desk,
or your life on a bus, or in a car,
or at the computer.

Not just your life of your mind,
but the life of your heart.
Not just your bank account,
but your Soul.

People don't talk about the soul
very much anymore.
It's so much easier to write a resume
than to craft a spirit.

But a resume is a cold comfort
on a winter night.
Or when you are sad,
or broke, or lonely.
Or when you've gotten back the test results
and they are not so good.

Here is my resume.
I am a good mother to three children.
I have tried never to let my profession
stand in the way of being a good parent.
I no longer consider myself
the center of the universe.

I show up
I listen
I try to laugh.

I am a good friend to my husband.
I have tried to make marriage vows
mean with they say.

I show up.
I listen.
I try to laugh.

I am a good friend to my friends
and they to me.
Without them,
there would be nothing to say to you today.,
because I would be a cardboard cutout.

But I call them on the phone,
and I meet them for lunch.

I show up.
I listen.
I try to laugh.

I would be rotten,
or at best mediocre at my job,
if those other things were not true.
You cannot be really first rate at your work
if your work is all you are.

So here's what I wanted to tell you today:
Get a Life.
A Real Life,
not a manic pursuit of the next promotion,
the bigger pay check,
the larger house.

Do you think you'd care
so very much about those things
if you blew an aneurysm one afternoon,
or found a lump in your breast?

Get a Life
in which you notice the smell of salt water
pushing itself
on a breeze over Seaside Heights,

A life in which you stop
and watch how a red-tailed hawk
circles over the water gap,
or the way a baby scowls with concentration
when she tries to pick of a Cheerio
with her thumb and first finger.

Get a Life in which you are not alone.
Find people you love, and who love you.
And remember
that love is not leisure,
It is work.

Each time you look at your diploma,
remember
that you are still a student,
still learning how to best treasure
your connection to others.

Pick up the phone.
Send an e-mail.
Write a letter.

Kiss your Mom.
Hug your Dad.

Get a Life in which you are generous.
Look around at the azaleas
in the neighborhood
where you grew up.
Look a t a full moon
hanging silver in a black,
black sky on a cold night.

And realize
that Life is the best thing ever,
and that you have
no business taking it for granted.

Care so deeply about life's goodness
that you want to spread it around.

Take money you would
have spent on beers
and give it to charity.
Work in a soup kitchen.
Be a Big Brother or Sister.

All of you want to do well.
But if you do not do good , too
then doing well
will never be enough.

It is so easy
to waste our lives:
Our days,
our hours,
our minutes.

It is so easy to take for granted
the color of the azaleas,
the color
of our kids' eyes,

The way a melody
in a symphony
rises and falls
and disappears
and rises again.

It is so easy to exist instead of live.

I learned to live many years ago.
Something really, really bad
happened to me,
Something that changed my life
in ways that,
if I had my druthers
It would never have been changed at all.

And what I learned from it
is what, today seems to be
the hardest lesson of all.

I learned to love the journey,
not the destination.
I learned that it is not
a dress rehearsal.
And that today
is the only guarantee you get.

I learned to look
at all the good in the world.
And to try
to give some of it back,
because I believed in it
completely and utterly.
And I tried to do that,
in part,
by telling others
what I had learned.

By telling them this:
Consider the lilies of the field.
Look at the fuzz on a baby's ear.
Read in the backyard with the
sun on your face.

Learn to be happy.
And think of life
as a terminal illness
Because if you do
you will live with joy and passion
as it ought to be lived.

Well, you can learn all those things,
Out there,
if you get a Real Life,
a full life.
A professional life, yes,
but another life ,too,

A life of love and laughs
and a connection
to other human beings.

Just keep your eyes
and ears open.
Here you could learn
in the classroom.

There the classroom
is everywhere.

The exam comes at the very end.
No man ever said on his deathbed
I wish I had spent more time at the office.

There are many things
in life that will catch your eye.-
But only a few
will catch your heart.
Pursue those.

Anna Quindlen

Villanova Commencement Address

Part IV
The Power Of Wisdom

Wisdom For The Journey

How High the Soul

The world stands out on either side
no wider than the heart is wide,
above the world is stretched the sky,
no higher than the soul is high.

Edna St.Vincent Millay

Wisdom

Wisdom is knowing what to do,
skill is knowing how to do it,
and virtue is doing it.

Anonymous

Journey of Faith

We are always traveling.

The journey of faith
is a little like a river.
It keeps flowing.
If it stops and stands still
it becomes stagnate.

Never give up in seeking faith
even in moments of fear,
moments of aloneness,
in moments of doubt.

We are all on different points
in the spectrum
in our relationship
with the spiritual.

We are seeking,
we are traveling.

We are always
on the journey.

Naomi Rosenblatt

Creating Happiness

I used to think you look for happiness.
Now I've decided, at 80,
you make and create your own.

When you're happy, other people feel good, too.
Don't fuss so much over yourself.
Learn to think less of yourself and more of others.
It's the little things we do for each other that counts.

The more you give,
the more you are happy.
and then there's no time for loneliness.

Grace Zia Chu

Thoughts and Words

If we want to be responsible for our lives,
we've got to be responsible for our words.

Our thoughts and words are very powerful,
and create our reality.
So let's choose them both with wisdom.

Louise L. Hay

Love of God

The love of God lies
in what we do, day by day.

And what we do,
when we do right
is not innate.

It must be taught.
It must be learned.

The great teachers and prophets
in every tradition,
have always pointed the way
to the conquest and rededication
of our very own nature.

Cynthia Ozick

Trying Too Hard

In any psychological or physical endeavor,
we know that trying too hard
usually generates so much tension
that it makes reaching the goal
even more difficult.

Happiness,
joy,
delight
in another.

These are things that cannot
be compulsively sought after.

They are the by-products of who you are
and how intelligently you have
developed your mind,
your heart,
and your spirit.

Marie Edwards and E. Hoover

Musical Score

My life continues
like a musical score,
always on
several lines at once.

Anais Nin

The Ebb and Flow of Life

We learn in waves,
not in upward linear lines.

There is an ebb and flow,
a rhythm to thought,
to learning patterns,
to life itself.

We climb upward
in thoughts and learning.
The wave crests,
then recedes.
We are at a resting plateau.

The ebb tide,
the time when thoughts
or things seem at a standstill,
at a low point,
is in reality a resting time.

A time to gather inner strength.
A time to hold to positive thoughts.
A time to be patient
and to affirm cosmic truths.

Then we move forward again.
with the flow of life.

Sonia Michelson

To Think Clearly

To have ideas is to gather flowers.
To think, is to weave them into garlands.

Madame Swetchine

Flexibility of Mind

What counts in the long run,
is not what you read.
It is what you sift though
your own mind.

It is the ideas stirred
in your own mind,
the ideas that are a reflection
of your own thinking,
which makes you an interesting person.

If we can keep that flexibility of mind,
that hospitality towards new ideas,
we will be able to welcome
the new flow of thought
from wherever it comes.

Not restricting it,
but weighing and evaluating
and exploring,
the strange new concepts
that confront us at every turn.

Eleanor Roosevelt

Something To Believe In

One needs something to believe in.
Something for which one can have
wholehearted enthusiasm.

Hannah Senesh

Coming Home

If we are to find a path of our own,
it helps to know and appreciate
the paths of others.

Women's spirituality
is about connectedness.

Appreciating both the hero's and heroine's journey,
the balance of female and male in ourselves,
our religions and the world.

Women can come home to themselves,
to communities of worship
and to God.

Joan Borysenko

Living and Learning

*Today living and learning
must go hand in hand.*

*Each new bit of knowledge,
each new experience.
is an extra tool
in meeting new problems
and working them out.*

Eleanor Roosevelt

Sudden Understanding

*That is what learning is.
You suddenly understand something
you've understood all your life,
but in a new way.*

Doris Lessing

An Open Mind

If you value wisdom,
you also value people continuing to develop.
You don't have much wisdom
if you close your mind and
don't learn anything new.

The wise people in society
are the people who can deal with change.

The people I admire most
are those with open minds,
and are learning new things
when they are quite old.

Margaret Mead

A Joyous Life

If we want a joyous life,
we must think joyous thoughts.
If we want a prosperous life,
we must think prosperous thoughts.
If we want a loving life,
we must think loving thoughts.
Whatever we send out mentally or verbally
will come back to us in like form.

Louise L. Hay

Grasping An Idea

A person is shown as clearly
by what he does not grasp,
as by what he does;
sometimes even more so.

Simone de Beauvoir

Facing Life

Life has to be faced.
to be rejected;
then accepted on new terms
with rapture.

Virginia Woolf

To Think

To think and to be fully alive are the same thing.
Man's chief moral deficiency appears to be
not his indiscretions but his reticence.

Hannah Arendt

Comes The Dawn

After awhile you learn the subtle difference
between holding a hand and chaining a soul,
and you learn that love doesn't mean leaning
and company doesn't mean security.

And you begin to learn that kisses aren't contracts
and presents aren't promises,
and you begin to accept your defeat
with your head up and your eyes open.

And you learn to build all your roads
on today
because tomorrow's ground
is too uncertain for plans, and futures have
a way of falling down in mid-flight.

After awhile you learn that even sunshine
burns if you get too much.

So you plant your own garden
and decorate your own soul ,
instead of waiting
for someone to bring you flowers.

And you learn that you really can endure
that you really are strong
and you really do have worth
and you learn and learn
with every goodbye you learn.

Anonymous

Seeing Through the Eyes of the Soul

The Divine is hidden from ordinary view,
but obvious to someone
who can see "through the eyes of the Soul."
To be able to recognize God in the small details of your life.

Mystical teachings, especially ones so sublime,
are meant to shake up your rational mind.
The mind in you, the harbor of the ego,
always wants answers to be obvious,
big, powerful and immediate.
You want problems to be solved your way
and always with the outcome favoring you.

Seeing "through the eyes of your Soul"
begins with appreciating that all the things
in your life have purpose and meaning.

Purpose and meaning are revealed through
the values of the soul.
Learning is a soul value.
Truth, courage, integrity, creativity,
self-respect are all soul values.
And a belief in one's own ability to navigate
through life's storms is also a soul value.

When you look at life through "those eyes"
you hear conversations differently.
Ordinary words enter you as inspiration.
A passage in a book grabs your attention
because it sparks an idea.
God comes through the
hidden passageways
that are everywhere.

Everything that you think is small
can suddenly become big
and deeply significant
because you perceive God
through the hidden details of your life.

Carolyn Myss

The Human Condition

I speak to the black experience,
but I am always talking about the human condition –
about what we can endure, dream, fail at, and still survive.

The main thing in one's own private world is
to try to laugh as much as you cry.

Maya Angelou

In The Service of Life

This is Mother Teresa's basic message.
We serve life not because it is broken,
but because it is holy.

We are servers of the wholeness
and the mystery in life.

I think I would go so far as to say
that fixing and helping may often
be the work of the ego,
and service the work of the soul.

They may look similar if you are
watching from the outside,
but the inner experience is different.
When we serve, the outcome
is often different too.

When you serve,
you see life as a whole.
From the perspective of service
we are all connected.

Lastly, fixing and helping are
the basis of curing but not healing.
Only service heals.

Rachel Naomi Remen, M.D.

Time Is A Dressmaker

Time is a dressmaker
specializing in alterations.

Most higher education is devoted to
affirming the traditions and origins of
an exiting elite
and transmitting them
to new members.

Mary Catherine Bateson

Life The Real Counselor

Life is the only real counselor;
wisdom unfiltered through personal experience
does not become a part of the moral tissue.

Life is either always a tight-rope
or a feather bed.
Give me the tight-rope.

Silence may be as variously
shaded as speech.

Time, when left to itself and
no definite demands are made on it,
cannot be trusted to move
at any recognized pace.
Usually it loiters,
but just when one has come
to count upon its slowness,
it may suddenly break
into a wild irrational gallop.

Edith Wharton

Importance of Solitude

Quiet Time Alone

Women must be the pioneers
in the turning inward for strength.

The answer for women today
is not in the feverish pursuit
of centrifugal activities
which only lead to fragmentation
of the personality.

William James describes it as
"Zerrisenheit"
(torn-to-pieces-hood).

Women today must consciously
encourage those pursuits
which oppose
the centrifugal forces of today.

Quiet time alone:
Contemplation,
Prayer,
Music.

A centering line of thought,
or reading, or study,
or work.

Any creative life proceeding
from oneself.

A woman must be still
as the axis of a wheel
in the midst of her activities.

She must keep the island-quality,
her core,
her center intact within her,
so that she may give to
those around her and
to the world at large.

Anne Morrow Lindbergh

God's Greatness

And I smiled to see God's greatness
flowed around our incompleteness.
Round our restlessness,
His rest.

Elizabeth Barrett Browning

Silence Within

Learn to get in touch
with the silence within you.

Know that everything
in this life has a purpose.

There are no mistakes,
no coincidences.

All events are blessings
given to us to learn from.

Elisabeth Kubler-Ross, M.D.

Let The Soul Rest

Let the soul rest.

I hardly ever sit still without being
haunted by the "undone."

I forget how important
the empty days are.

A day where one has not
pushed oneself to the limit
seems a damaged day,
a sinful day.

Not so.

The most valuable
thing we can do
for the psyche, occasionally,
is to let it rest.

Wander.
Live in the changing
light of the room.

Not trying to be or
do anything whatever.

May Sarton

The Journey

I hoped that the trip
would be the best
of all journeys:
A journey into ourselves.

Shirley MacLaine

Loneliness Is Part of Living

Have I ever been lonely?
Loneliness is a part of living.
We will never lose it.

People find it in the midst of crowds.
A certain amount of loneliness
is inherent in the human condition.

Reverend Dr. Pauli Murray

When One is Alone

Actually these are among the
most important times in one's life,
when one is alone.

Certain springs are tapped
only when we are alone.

The artist knows he must be alone
to create;
the writer, to work out his thoughts;
the musician, to compose;
the saint to pray.

But women need solitude
in order to find again
the true essence of themselves:

The firm strand which will
be the indispensable center
of a whole web of
human relationships.

She must find the inner stillness
which Charles Morgan describes as the
"stilling of the soul...
within the activities of mind and body.

so that it might be
still as the axis of a
revolving wheel is still."

One needs to still the soul
in the midst of its activities.

Anne Morrow Lindbergh

Renewing Your Inner Springs

I love people.
I love my family, my children.

But inside myself is a place
where I live all alone.

And that's where you renew
your springs
that never dry up.

Pearl S. Buck

Solitude

Being solitary is being alone well.
Being alone immersed in
doings of your own choice.

Aware of the fullness of your
own presence
rather than the absence of others.

Because solitude is an achievement.
It is your distinctive way
of embodying the purposes
you have chosen for your life.

Above all,
finding inner
as well as outer solitude
may be the most honest
way of living.

It's not only genuinely
being by oneself
but becoming oneself.

Alice Koller

Creative Aging

Needed: A Model For Aging

*Gloria Steinem reflects on changing
in mid-stream in her 50th year.*

*The everyday emergencies of a magazine
and a movement were all-consuming,
and I didn't think I could stop
swimming in mid-stream.*

*But to a larger degree,
I just didn't know how.
I didn't have a model of
how to get from here (at 50)
to there;
from where I was
to seventy, eighty and hopefully beyond.*

*I needed a model
not of being old, but of aging.*

Gloria Steinem

Have No Regrets

I consider it an essential preparation for old age,
not to have any regrets.

We rarely regret the things we do.
If you make a mistake,
you don't have to regret it
because you learn from it.

Even if your mistake hurts other people,
it still means that from that point on,
you can bring greater sensitivity and compassion
to your relationships with others.

"Always try everything twice."

That's sound advice at any age.

Eda LeShan

Accepting Life On New Terms

Life has to be sloughed:
has to be faced
has to be rejected.
Then accepted on
new terms with rapture.

And so on, and so on;
until you are 40,
when the only problem is
how to grasp it tighter
and tighter to you,
so quick it seems to slip,
and so infinitely desirable is it.

Virginia Woolf

Age

We are always
the same age
inside.

Gertrude Stein

Life Has Got To Be Lived

Life has got to be lived!
That's all there is to it.

At 70 I would say that the advantage is that
you take life more calmly.
You know that "this too, shall pass."

Eleanor Roosevelt

On Aging

Old age is like a plane
flying through a storm.
Once you are aboard
there is nothing you
can do about it.

Golda Meir

Cultural Conditioning

What an individual believes
is heavily influenced by the culture
in which she lives.

If we can leap out of the cultural jar
and limiting mind sets
and assumptions about how
one is "supposed to grow old"
we might have a greater chance of replacing
years of decline with
years of growth and purpose .

Dr. Ellen Langer

Commitment

Never doubt that a small group of thoughtful,
committed people can change the world.
Indeed it is the only thing that ever has.

Margaret Mead

The Old-Old

People want things to go well, but they are human.
Everybody steps on everybody's toes.
There is baggage from the past
between generations,
as well as trouble in the present.

Our parents were not perfect parents
and we were not perfect children.

Nobody becomes perfect with age.
Loving people sometimes
means disappointment.

Old age can be a time of great sorrow
but also a time of great healing.
Successful resolution of this stage
allows the old-old to feel respected
and at peace with their families.

They learn to accept the nurturing that
children offer.
The young get the chance to
grow up and truly be adults.

*We can learn a great deal
from the old-old.
They can teach us the
importance of Time,
Relationships,
and Gratitude.
They can teach us
how to endure and
how to be patient.*

Mary Pipher

Getting Older

*The great thing about getting older
is that you don't lose
all the other ages you've been.*

Madeline L'Engle

Appreciating Our Elders

Our elders can teach us about
Creativity,
Accountability,
Connection.
Their knowledge of how to
tell stories, how to live together,
how to nurture children,
how to share the work.
All this knowledge will
help to build better
connections for the future.

Mary Pipher

People Over 65

The Gray Panthers are bringing a special message
to the people over sixty-five:

"Look, you have the freedom to initiate change."

We felt that, as older people,
we had the freedom to do
what needed to be done.
This was one aspect of preparation
for the new stage of retirement.

You don't retire from life.
You just recycle and redirect your goals.

Maggie Kuhn

Role Model

The best thing you can do for your
friends or your family,
is to be an example
through your recovery.

You will be a bridge
that will allow others
to cross from self-doubt
to self-expression.

Julia Cameron

The Resilient Old

The resilient old carry on
in spite of losses.

They tend to be practical
and sensible and well-organized.

All have interests and relationships
that sustain them.

They are appreciative, and grateful
for a fresh muffin,
a call from a friend or a grandchild.

They discover pleasure in small moments.

The old have discovered independently
the same Truth –
that acceptance is the key to serenity.

That gratitude is the
key to happiness.

Mary Pipher

Our Blessings

The capacity to bless life is in everybody.
The power of our blessing is not
diminished by illness or age.

On the contrary,
our blessings become
even more powerful as
we grow older.

They have survived the
buffeting of our experience.

We have traveled a long, hard
road to the place where we
can remember once again
who we are.

That we have traveled
and remembered,
gives hope to
those we bless.
To this place where we
belong to one another.

Rachel Naomi Remen, M.D.

Reach Out To Others

Now I'm traveling with a new kind of freedom and purpose.
I tell older people who are feeling lonely and depressed
to stop thinking about themselves.

Unless you reach out to an ever-widening community,
circles that continue to expand,
then your old age, when the primary circle contracts,
you may be the only survivor.

If all through your life you've been
wrapped up in your family,
and then they die,
and you've never developed any facility
or any feeling of competence,
you're stuck with yourself---
stuck with your own memories,
your own anger, your own angst.

You think you have no future,
only a lonely, miserable present.
And you make everyone else
around you miserable too.

Young and old can
and should work together
for social change.

Their needs and concerns
are not mutually exclusive.

Maggie Kuhn (at age 74)

Life's Wisdom

Life offers its wisdom generously.
Everything teaches.
Stay Awake. Pay Attention.
It requires us not to be distracted by:

- *expectations*
- *past experiences*
- *labels*
- *masks*
- *not jump to early conclusions*
- *remain open to surprises*

Have the courage to embrace life
without judgment,
with a willingness to "not know"
sometimes for a long time.
A greater "wholeness" is possible.

Rachel Naomi Remen, M.D.

Advice to Older and Younger Generations

Mary Pipher in her book Another Country:
Navigating the Emotional Terrain of Our Elders
offers good advice gleaned from her many interviews
with elders, many of them in their 70s and 80s.

- *Find good work and a purpose in life.*

- *Find people to love.*

- *Focus on the positives in life.*

- *Appreciate small things.*

- *Don't cross your bridges until you come to them.*

- *Be optimistic.*

- *Feel the way you think.*

- *Some things are better left unsaid.*

- *Silence is also an answer.*

- *"Don't Go There" is really a warning*
  not to process a particular experience.

- *Flexibility works best.*

- *The importance of character and taking responsibility.*

- *Be honest and open about feelings. Speak up.*

- *Find the golden mean, the middle way.*

- *Try to turn sorrow into wisdom.*

- *A sense of humor is very important and so is laughter.*

Respect For Age

I don't hide my age.
Just because I'm eighty,
I'm not an old lady.
I just do less.
I used to do three, four,
or five things at the same time.
I don't anymore.

The Chinese like to be older.
There is respect for older people.

I think people should face old age.
They should talk about it,
plan for it.

Grace Zia Chu (at age 80)

A Good Routine

*It's good to have routines and
it's good to violate them.*

*The old must search for the right
mix of comfortable habits and
new experiences.*

*Without the former
there is chaos.
Without the latter
there is ossification.*

Mary Pipher

Learning New Things

*If you value Wisdom, you also value people continuing to develop.
You don't have much wisdom if you close your mind
and don't learn anything new.*

*The wise people in society are the people who can deal with change.
The people I admire most are those with Open Minds
and are learning new things when they are quite old.*

Margaret Mead

Beauty From the Inside Out

On the American Woman

It is a strangely disquieting phenomenon,
this focus on youth in America.
In France,
a woman is not considered beautiful
until she is forty.
It takes at least that long for the true character,
the inner description of life
to manifest itself physically,
so that a woman can be known
to be beautiful from the inside out.

Patricia Kennedy Helman

Integrity at 80

Even after many years seeing,
thinking and living one way,
we may be able to reach past all that
to claim our integrity.
And live in a way we may never
have expected to live.

Rachel Naomi Remen, M.D.

Enthusiasm

A t age 70, Ruth Gordon said,
"Keep enthusiastic all the time.
After 65, I published my first two books..."

I have begun to learn the lesson we all need to learn;
that ultimately and forever each of us is alone.
We are born alone and we die alone,
no matter how close we are to other people.

And if there is one single thing we need
in order to face our later years,
it is to find pleasure in that companionship.

Eda LeShan

Moving Ahead

When Gloria Steinem turned 60 at a surprise party she said:

"The victory is not just hanging on to what you already have
or against all onslaughts,
but going on to something different and better."

Gail Sheehy

Facing Fear and Crisis

Facing Fear

You gain strength, courage
and confidence
by every experience
in which you really stop
to look fear in the face.

You must do the thing
you think you cannot do.
This brings confidence and success.

Eleanor Roosevelt

Understanding Life

Nothing in life is to be feared.
It is only to be understood.

Marie Curie

Grasp Every Opportunity

Every time you meet a crisis and live through it,
you make it simpler for the next time.
It requires effort to use all your potentialities
to the best of your ability,
to stretch your horizon,
to grasp every opportunity as it comes.

Very often people seem afraid
to put their own capabilities to use,
as though one could save one's abilities
and draw interest on them.
The only interest, of course, comes from spending.

Or they believe that if they make use of their own assets,
some demands will be made upon them.
Some people never dare
to find out how much they are really capable of doing.

By trying to do something new,
you free yourself from a fear,
and stretch your mental muscles
and gain the freedom that comes with achievement.

Eleanor Roosevelt

Trust in God

*One of the problems all parents face
is that of bringing up their children
to be as free of fear as possible.*

*If you can give them trust in God
they will have one sure way
of meeting all the uncertainties
of existence.*

Eleanor Roosevelt

Learn To Sail Your Own Ship

I'm not afraid of storms,
for I'm learning how to sail my own ship.
I do not ask for any crown
but that which all may win;
Nor try to conquer any world
except the one within.
Be Thou my guide until I find
led by a tender hand,
the happy kingdom in myself
and dare to take command.

Louisa May Alcott

Inner Wisdom: Intuition

A Woman's Spiritual Nature

Women need to connect deeply with their spiritual nature.
They need to know that no matter what the culture says,
an endless supply of spiritual energy is available to guide their lives.

Once you've tuned in to your inner wisdom,
you can start to live from the heart.
Then life begins to fall into place
in an organic way that's very serendipitous.

Christiane Northrup, M.D.

Neuro-Peptides

A part of your body's wisdom is its ability to respond
to your thoughts and emotions,
which have very real biochemical consequences.
This means that your positive emotions, like joy,
tend to enhance your immune functions,
while chronic, unexpressed emotions like anger and resentment,
tend to do the opposite,
damper your immune response.

Amazing as it seems, every thought you think
and every emotion you feel
communicates to each cell in your body through the
language of tiny protein molecules
messengers known as neuro-peptides.

Your emotions have enormous power to create health.

Christiane Northrup, M.D.

Mind and Soul

The mind and the soul, which permeate our entire body,
are much vaster than the intellect can possibly grasp.
Our inner guidance comes to us through
our feelings and body wisdom first,
not through intellectual understanding.
The intellect works best in service to our intuition,
our inner guidance, Soul, or Higher Power,
the spiritual energy that animates our life.

Christiane Northrup, M.D.

Our Many Selves

We are so many selves.
It's not just the long-ago child within us
who needs tenderness and inclusion,
but the person we were last year,
wanted to be yesterday.

What brings together these ever-shifting selves
of infinite reaction and returning is this:
There is always one true inner voice.
Trust it.

Gloria Steinem

Wisdom to Befriend Life

The wisdom to befriend life will find us,
whether or not we pursue it.

We may live in a familiar circle of
experience for many years among

- *attitudes*
- *beliefs*
- *places*
- *relationships*

that define our everyday world.

It is only a matter of Time until
something invites or requires us
to reach beyond the familiar.

To experience something never before
felt or seen.
The experience can break open our sense
of what the world is about
and draw our attention to who we are!

Such experience usually involves
either Suffering or Joy.

Both Suffering and Joy will leave us wiser.

Rachel Naomi Remen, M.D.

Inner Wisdom

What is your body's "inner wisdom?"

I mean your body's subtle guidance system
that communicates with you
through your physical and emotional health.

Often, illness is a message
that something in our lives is out of balance.
Fortunately your body also has the "wisdom"
to very often heal itself and guide you towards health.

Christiane Northrup, M.D.

Awareness

As a woman I believe in the great importance of faith,
the importance of orientation and the inner life
to withstand outer pressures.

Also the understanding, that increased awareness
will prevail and cause external changes.
The importance of inner conviction.
I had the love of my work and nothing could stop it.

Anais Nin

Grow in Wisdom

We are here to grow in wisdom.
to learn how to love better.

As each of us do this
in our own ways,
we slowly become
a blessing to those around us.
And a Light in the world.

Rachel Naomi Remen, M.D.

Character

Gift

Gift,
like Genius,
I often think,
means only an
infinite capacity
for taking pains.

Jane E. Hopkins

The Right Path

Parents can only give good advice,
or put them on the right paths,
but the final forming of a
person's character
lies in their own hands.

Anne Frank

Vigorous Minds

Great character is formed
not in the calm of life
but in times of tension and stress.
The habits of vigorous minds are formed
in contending with difficulties.

Abagail Adams
Letter to son, President John Quincy Adams

What Remains To Be Done

I never see what has to be done,
I only see,
what remains to be done.

Marie Curie

Our Deeds

Our deeds
determine us,
as much as we
determine our deeds.

George Eliot

Bibliographic Index

Bibliographic Index

A

Hannah Arendt (1906-1995) – American German historian and political philosopher. p. 63, 71.

Abigail Adams (1744-1818) – First Lady to President John Adams and Mother of John Quincy Adams, 6th President of the United States. p. 59, 73.

Miriam Adahan – American-born Israeli psychologist and author of Appreciating People (Including Yourself). p. 25.

Grace Aguilar – Nineteenth century British author who wrote books for women. p. 25.

Gina Allen – American author. p. 45.

Louisa May Alcott (1832-1888) – American author of Little Women. p. 23, 83, 200.

Maya Angelou – American writer, poet, performer and director. Author of I Know Why The Caged Bird Sings and The Complete Poems of Maya Angelou. p. 167.

Jane Austen – English author of Pride and Prejudice and Sense and Sensibility. p. 61, 69.

B

Pearl S. Buck (1892-1973) – American novelist and author of The Good Earth. She was a Nobel Laureate for Literature. p. 19, 80, 177.

Ruth Benedict (1887-1948) American anthropologist and author of Patterns of Culture. p. 104.

Elizabeth Barrett Browning (1806-1861) – English poet, author of Sonnets from the Portuguese and wife of the poet Robert Browning. p. 23, 173.

E

Marie Edwards and Elaine Hoover – American journalists. p. 73, 155.

Amelia Earheart (1898-1937) – American pioneer aviator and the first woman to cross the Atlantic in a solo flight in 1931. p. 70, 71, 110, 113.

George Eliot (1819-1880) – Pseudonym for Mary Ann Evans. She was an English writer and novelist. Her best known books are Adam Bede, Mill on the Floss and Middlemarch. p. 78, 80, 106, 125.

Marion Edelman – Attorney, social activist who began the Children's Defense Fund. Author of The Measure of Our Success: A Letter to My Children and Yours. p. 53, 136.

Donna Eden – Pioneer American energy medicine healer and author of Energy Medicine, with David Feinstein Ph.D. p. 90.

F

Anne Frank (1929-1945) – Young Jewish heroine diarist. She was a concentration camp victim during World War II. She died at age 14 after having written her famous book The Diary of Anne Frank while hiding from the Nazis with her family in Holland. p 11, 54.

Dame Margot Fonteyn (1919-1999) – English dancer who became on of the greatest ballerinas of the twentieth century. p. 134.

G

Martha Graham (1894-1991) – Dancer and choreographer who developed a radically new approach to modern dance. p. 134.

Emma Goldman (1869-1940) – Russian-American social activist, nurse and propagandist who wrote Living My Life. p. 74.

Dr. Lillian M. Gilbreth – A noted engineer in the early twentieth century. She was also widely known as mother-heroine of the book Cheaper By The Dozen. p. 13.

H

Yitta Halberstam and Judith Leventhal – American authors of Small Miracles. p. 26, 55.

Louise L. Hay – American metaphysical author of You Can Heal Your Life and founder of Hay House Publishers. p. 31, 153, 162.

Katherine Hepburn – Oscar-winning American actress. p. 77.

Marilyn Horne – Mezzo-Soprano superstar who sang in operas and recitals. p. 79.

Lillian Helman (1905-1984) – Playwright and acclaimed author of The Little Foxes and Watch On The Rhine. p. 127.

K

Elisabeth Kubler-Ross, M.D. – Swiss-born psychiatrist and writer, famous for pioneering research into the experience of dying. She wrote On Death and Dying and Death the Final Stage. p. 26, 54, 103, 124, 173.

Helen Keller (1880-1968) – American author and lecturer. Blind and deaf from infancy she was taught to speak and read Braille. She was the first deaf- blind person to earn a bachelor of arts degree and to graduate from Radcliff College. She inspired and influenced countless thousands by her writings, her courage and indomitable will. She was the author of many books, including her first book written at age twenty-two The Story of My Life. p. 11, 16, 21, 105, 133, 137.

Alice Koller – American author, p. 178.

Maggie Kuhn (1905-1995) – American social activist and national convener of the Gray Panthers. A prolific writer she also worked for nursing home reforms and fought ageism. p. 187, 190.

L

Ellen Langer, Ph.D – Professor of Psychology at Harvard University, and the author of Mindfulness and Counter-Clockwise. p. 183.

Frances Moore Lappe – *Author of Diet for a Small Planet the ground-breaking book about a new way of eating with emphasis on nutrition on a global level. p. 15.*

Eda LeShan – *American psychologist, and author of The Wonderful Crisis of Middle Age. p. 40, 50, 97, 99, 115, 124, 128, 133, 180, 196.*

Doris Lessing – *American Rhodesian writer and novelist who wrote The Golden Notebook and Love Again. p. 160.*

Anne Morrow Lindbergh (1906-2001) – *American author and aviator who wrote Gift From The Sea reflections on a woman's life in the midst of her activities as wife, mother, writer and aviator. p. 27, 56, 72, 100, 112, 121, 126, 172, 176.*

Elise Michelson Levin – *American born-Israeli nurse and mid-wife. p. 24, 53.*

Harriet Lerner, Ph.D – *Psychologist and author of On Mothers and Daughters. p. 39.*

M

Golda Meir (1898-1978) – *Russian-American-Israeli politician and Israel's fourth Prime Minister. p. 19, 182.*

Caroline Myss – *American Medical Intuitive, lecturer and author of Anatomy of the Spirit. p. 31, 165.*

Margaret Mead (1901-1978) – *American anthropologist and author of Coming of Age in Samoa and Male and Female. p. 44, 38, 161, 183,194.*

Catherine Marshall – *American author and lecturer. p. 115.*

Shirley MacLaine – *Oscar-winning American actress, dancer and writer. Author of Dance While You Can and Out On A Limb. p. 175.*

Sonia Michelson – *Teacher, writer, editor and author of New Dimensions in Classical Guitar for Children, Young Beginner's First Repertoire for Classic Guitar, Home At Last: My First Year in Israel, and Wise Women: Wise Words: Empowering Words of Wisdom by Women. p. 34, 43, 81, 87, 156.*

Rev. Dr. Pauli Murray – American priest, lawyer and novelist. She is the first African-American woman to become an Episcopal priest. p. 125, 175.

Edna St. Vincent Milay (1892-1950) – She is best known for Renaissance and Other Poems. p. 63, 151.

Toni Morrison – Writer, teacher, editor and novelist. She was a Pulitzer Prize winner for her novel Beloved, and the first African-American woman to receive the Nobel Prize for Literature. p. 80, 117.

N

Louise Nevelson (1900-1988) – American sculptor, famous for her boxed assemblages and constructions of wood and steel. p. 107.

Christiane Northrop, M.D. – American holistic physician and well-known author of Women's Bodies, Women's Wisdom. Dr. Northrop writes with compassion and a new vision for women's health, well-being, joy and fulfillment. p. 29, 30, 37, 42, 69, 85, 87, 91, 92, 105, 108, 135, 201, 202, 203, 205.

Anais Nin – French-American diarist, author and lecturer. p. 59, 102, 118, 156.

O

Georgia O'Keefe (1887-1986) – Innovative American painter whose vibrant flowers and canvases with desert vistas made her unique as an aesthetic pioneer. p. 62.

Cynthia Ozick – American novelist, poet and writer. Among her books are The Shawl and Puttermesser Papers. p. 154.

P

Susan Page – American author of The Shortest Distance Between You and a Published Book. p. 22.

Mary Pipher, Ph.D. – Internationally noted psychologist and author of Another Country: Navigating the Emotional Terrain of Our Elders. p. 12, 18, 41, 144, 146, 148, 192, 194.

Q

Anna Quindlen – American author of One True Thing and Black and Blue and acclaimed former journalist of the New York Times. p. 138.

R

Eleanor Roosevelt (1884-1962) – Inspiring and much admired international humanitarian, author of many books including You Learn By Living. She was First Lady of the United States and delegate to the United Nations. p. 16, 57, 67, 70, 77, 83, 95, 98, 108, 130, 158, 160, 182, 197, 198, 199.

Sonya Richmond – American author of Common Sense About Yoga. p. 28, 131.

Klara Roman – Hungarian-American psychologist and handwriting expert. p. 68, 109.

Nancy Roberts – American journalist. p. 110.

Naomi Rosenblatt, Israeli-American psychotherapist, lecturer and author of In God's Image. p. 152.

Rachel Naomi Remen M.D. – Co-founder and Medical Director of the Commonweal Cancer Center in California and author of Kitchen Table Wisdom and My Grandfather's Blessings. p. 101, 122, 168, 189, 191, 195, 201, 206.

S

George Sand (1801-1876) – Pseudonym for Amadine Aurore Lucie Dupin, Baroness Dudevant, French novelist and playwright. p. 17, 65.

Gloria Steinem, Internationally acclaimed American writer, feminist and social reformer and author of Revolution From Within: A Book of Self Esteem. p. 21, 72, 74, 103, 104, 121, 127, 179, 203.

Gail Sheehy – American journalist and author of Passages and Pathfinders. p. 36, 75, 96, 103, 129, 196.

Barbara Seaman – American author of Free and Female p. 123.

About the Author

Sonia Michelson is the author of a critically acclaimed method for teaching young children, *New Dimensions in Classical Guitar for Children.* She has also published *Easy Classic Guitar Solos* and *Young Beginner's First Repertoire for Classical Guitar.*

At the age of seventy-seven she decided to move her home and classical guitar studio from Los Angeles to Israel. She now lives in Ofra, Israel near her family.

Her previous books also include *Home at Last: My First Year in Israel* and *With T L C II: A Memoir – Cookbook* in both English and Hebrew as a legacy for her children, grandchildren and great-grandchildren living in Israel and in the United States.